MEPHISTOS
& OTHER POEMS

MEPHISTOS
& OTHER POEMS

MICHAEL ★ McCLURE

City Lights Books | San Francisco

Library of Congress Cataloging-in-Publication Data
Names: McClure, Michael, author.
Title: Mephistos and other poems / Michael McClure.
Description: San Francisco : City Lights Publishers, [2016]
Identifiers: LCCN 2016020216 | ISBN 9780872867284 (softcover)
Subjects: | BISAC: POETRY / American / General. | LITERARY
COLLECTIONS /
  American / General. | NATURE / Ecology.
Classification: LCC PS3563.A262 A6 2016 | DDC 811/.54—dc23
LC record available at https://lccn.loc.gov/2016020216

Some of these poems first appeared in: *The New Yorker, London Review of Books, Milk Mag, Page Boy, Cafe Review, Vanitas, Capillano Review, Zen Monster, From the Tower, Homage to Etel Adnan, Eleven Eleven,* and *Clark. An Anthology of Clark County Poetry*

City Lights Books are published at the City Lights Bookstore
261 Columbus Avenue, San Francisco, CA 94133
www.citylights.com

CONTENTS

FOR THE PROTECTION OF ALL BEINGS

WITH DEEP HEART'S LOVE FOR
AMY JANE BILL JAMES MICHAEL

★ ★ ★ ★

once this was all black plasma
and imagination

FOREWORD

The world puts off its mask of vastness to its lover. It becomes small as one song, as one kiss of the eternal.
— Rabindranath Tagore

The flow of energery through the system acts to organize the system.
— Harold Morowitz

A mouse is miracle enough to stagger sextillions of infidels.
— Walt Whitman

The poems in *Mephistos* are written in Projective Verse — a mode that is neither metrical nor free verse. Projective Verse is a style that gives swift access of the energy of inspiration to the Heart where it bounces through the syllable to the Breath and onto the field of composition.

Some poems here are written spontaneously and without changes and others are lengthily studied.

"All art should become science and all science art; poetry and philosophy should be made one."

These words of Friedrich Schlegel are not less true in these times of Projective Verse and of new poetry and witnessing investigations of dances in living protein.

These poems celebrate art, biology, imagination and inspiration, and I thank my gifted friends who have brought me to them.

The poems in *Mephistos* are like the energy of consciousness moving vertically on a scroll or screen. Look at them as you would look at calligraphy. They are for the voice and the eye.

If the type and placement of lines seem strange, read them aloud and they will take their shape.

Capitalized lines are not to be read louder.

Single-letter lines gliding down the page, move normally as breath does.

Poetry is a muscular principle.

*

1.
Emily Dickinson writes that Mephistopheles would be the best friend if he had fidelity. If so, he would then be "thoroughly divine." Mephistopheles, the soul-thief, returns aged and exhausted Faust to his inspiration, energy, and sexuality. Mephistopheles is an active and witty companion for an inspired journey. He scatters treachery and tricks, and is finally foiled.

Mephisto (the same name) is an angel who helps God in constructing the universe and in the creation of orcas and giant sea mammals.

2.
The thirty-seven strophes of *Mephistos* resemble a medicine bundle. American Indians gathered spirit objects to make medicine bundles that they carried along, whether in the heart or in a pouch. One bundle I have seen is wrapped in a green-dyed otter skin.

Everything of *Mephistos* is happening or happened in the world or imagination, sensory prehension, or dreams.

Mephistos time-dive like dolphins through times and places in the sea of experience and imagination and do not have boundaries of grammar.

5.

Poems want to be real as the open face of a rose or the black smell of tar in the street.

6.

Mephistos celebrates our human-mammal love of nature and abhors the exuberant passion for its destruction. We are in the extreme slow motion explosion, and the *exponential* explosion, of forests and river-beds. Underground fuels, oceans, and atmosphere are in the blast that morphs them into world-size cinders of concrete and plastics — (our) cities and newly created deserts.

"Nature loves to hide herself," Heraclitus wrote in his fragments. This is the newest disguise.

7.

Some Fringes are small poems appearing from my love of haiku. They shed the rules of haiku and make shapes of perceptions and experiences. They are often funny and sometimes grand.

Experiences may be so tiny, so without scale or proportion that they would not exist without a *fringe* which flits like the blue-gray wing of a moth. Or like a coyote leaping across the highway, in front of my speeding car, and into the beach dunes.

8.

Each day for seventeen days, after sitting meditation, I wrote spontaneously. The ornament of those experiences is *Rose Breaths*, which is itself many experiences.

"The animal is in the world like water in water" is taken from Leslie Scalapino, who found it in the writing of Georges Bataille.

9.

My lifelong friend, Zen master Dave Haselwood, would not agree with my bleak view of hyper-reality in *The Surge*.

10.

The poem for Etel Adnan was written while reading her *Journey to Mount Tamalpais*. My memories of the mountain include seeing it every day and illegally camping there up high in a hidden nook with Freewheelin Frank, secretary of the Angels, smelling the wild odors and campfires, and listening to other secret campers in their nooks, and seeing wild stars and hearing foxes barking.

11.

Sestina for Amy is a bow to Troubadour Arnaut Daniel, inventor of the sestina form, which seems to be like a rose quartered. The sestina helps guide thoughts to be reborn and to be myriad. (Troubadour Arnaut Daniel may have found his inspiration in pre-Islamic Arabic poetry.)

12.

Pollock's Echo reflects Jackson Pollock's unexpected black and white paintings of 1951 in which he portrays the Beloved. I imagine his *Echo* painting laid out over a wall or hanging in space — it is like a moth wing pattern or the map of a woman. Pollock's woman, the Beloved, has stepped from the veils of his dripped skeins.

Novalis wrote this opening line: "The beloved is an abbreviation of the universe..."

and Jackson Pollock's heart is the
thin black enamel
of the birth of a rose
with the fragrance of flesh,
the mesh can never be lost...

(We're the net holding
ourselves and may again
be songbirds in a coal mine

Pastoral gorgeousness
pours from the stars,
through and back again,
going and ongoing
from the lip of the vessel

I
YOU

WE

the splashes

13.
The original of *Skaagi the Salmon* is in the art of Bill Reid, sculptor, artist, and *reinventor* of the Haida Indian style.

14.
Anacreon's Cupid and *Anacreon Meeting Cupid* refer to Anacreon whose extant lyrics sing of voluptuousness and wine. He is a poet of sixth-century B.C. Greece. A statue of drunken Anacreon stood on the Acropolis.

15.
One More Cherub in Honey is a strophe I read with Terry Riley playing piano at the San Francisco Jazz Center.

*

Mephisto 2: The elephant seal, or sea elephant, is enormous; bulls may weigh more than two tons. They have an elongated proboscis and make huge roars during bloody mating battles. The seals have a rookery on the coast of Northern California.

Mephisto 10: Psyche is the mind, or consciousness, and darts like a butterfly. Psyche was the butterfly-winged wife of Eros.

Mephisto 11: Odin, the father god of the Norse, plucked out his eye and threw it into All-Knowing Mimir's well in exchange for wisdom.

Mephisto 13: In his philosophy Heraclitus declares "panta rei," all things and happenings are in motion and flow like a river.

Mephisto 26: Dharmadatu, a term from Mahayana Buddhism meaning the uncaused nature of all presences and non-presences.

Mephisto 31: SAMSARA, the world of phenomena.

Mephisto 37: Ashvaghosha is a poet and philosopher of the second century A.D., one of the Buddhist saints and author of *The Divine Love and Wisdom*.

MEPHISTOS

MEPHISTO 1

NOW I UNDERSTAND THE SEXUAL ADDICTION
of my young manhood
was a CRUCIFIXION
glittering and lovely
as the smile of Mephisto
through a realm of rosy smoke
rising from a bonfire of future loves.
Just that simple.
— REAL FLESH
beginning to imagine
big crises where plain toes could step.
I love you,
YOU.
The red amaryllis and the lily
shake lightly in the car roar
above trees in sunset
and there's the beat of virility through old
and new muscles.
It's the blossom
of a spiritual occasion,
shadowlessly clear,
physical,
unforgiving
as truth
or a new poem.

Pleasure is the answer.

MEPHISTO 2

MY
GOD   MY GOD!

NO   MY GOD!

Don't   MY GOD!

DO
THIS

to me!

I am a thousand years
making an old man.

ALL
OF
THE
MOMENTS OF THIS
pleasure are just one. Made of the flesh
of your shoulders, and your eyes
looking up at me.
Your sloping breasts
and pink nipples sail
like little ships over my erection.
The vast elephant seal on the dark gray sand
in the crash of green-white, translucent breakers
by the ragged black rocks
is a body of hope for future
sexuality

and tiny sand pipers rush
in the shallow ripples.

MEPHISTO 3

"INCOMMENSURABLE
and incomprehensible are the best of poetic creation,"
the old man sings. The galaxies are a river
seen from this direction. The child knows
it is all black behind the eyes
and that flesh is a swirl,
whirling out of the nothingness
as I hear your toes' voice
and the muffled hoots
of an owl in the morning canyon.
The burning smell of frankincense
creates the room
and blue, red and opal cars
create the freeway.
I chase a giraffe
(IN KENYA)
as it runs with long,
stiff-legged strides
looking
back
at
me
without fear,
— and there is
A TURQUOISE
stone
in my hand.

THERE
IS
JOY
IN
THE
ROOM
sometimes it is solid
for a sixtieth of a second.
Moments supercede the pain of muscles
and Laughter is the prince of the gods.
This is ordinary as tiny green frogs,
perfectly striped
with black, and knowing,
and)) mindless eyes
in the marshy field grass.
Neighbors are close
and there is a scarlet fire
in the fireplace.

IT IS FEARSOME
to have intelligence threaten.

The calico cat hides, waiting
TO RUSH AT ME
in a gallop. Now her eyes
are aglint with delight,
in the midst of her dash,
as she slides on two paws
around the hall corner.

MEPHISTO 5

I AM A GOD WITH A HUGE FACE. Lions
and eagles pour out of my mouth. Big white
square teeth and a red-purple tongue. There are
magenta clouds around my head and this
is my throne room where I
change opals into souls
in a spark of alchemy.
Only a fool is impartial
to cool mist
on the face on a brisk walk
through the canyon. — Sometimes passed
in semi darkness by a biker
or
a car
delivering the papers.

AN

ORDINARY DAY
in Paradiso with clouds
of angels making a rose.

Smell of wet humus
over the rostrum of lichens.

We are "safe in Heaven dead"
and the drone planes do not film
our home for the watchers
near Denver.

MEPHISTO 6

SOMBREROS THE COLOR OF CHIDREN"S
COOKIES. Colorlessness at the edges
of things. — Radiances of blue-silver
roll through consciousness
past the precipice of protein and quarks.
The silk scarf is sleek
on
the
neck
— greens and reds melt into sienna.

ART
DISAPPEARS
in department store limbo.

I am always here on this rock
ESCARPEMENT
eating a sandwich with you,
watching mist tufts rise
from the ravines.

When you are angry
MY
CHEST,
these ribs,
lock together into stone
and there's the smell
of the smoke
of feathers burning.

MEPHISTO 7

VAN GOGH, DRAWING,
must have felt like this. The hunter
throws the chipped stone hand axe. Flint
and obsidian. The spirit rises from blood
AND TURNS, toward
or away from,
DOMESTICATION.
Let us be trackers in the realms
of these sweet plain streets.
Secret deer
look up from chewing
as muddy repair trucks
fix phone wires.
Over
the
hill
three flying ravens
are raucous.

MY PSYCHE
IS AS
TORN APART
as the amputated
four year old black boy,
with bandage over his stump shoulder.
WE
STARE
blank, bewildered, open eyed,
at the seething stew.
And I am a prince.

MEPHISTO 8

YOU ARE MY MEMORIES OF YOU
holding my hand
I
WANT
TO
GO
I want to go, I want to go
and come back
TO
YOU
where there is a solid mass
of galaxies around us.
We are storms of February flowers
and not puzzled children.
The strength of a forearm muscle
and sunlight
are
COURAGE
and
TRUTH.
(Real.)
I
HOLD
THEM
for fractious instants
of a horse neighing whinnying
in the murky paddock.

Fires are everywhere
in the rain.

ALL IS LIKE
t
h
i
s
.

MEPHISTO 9

YOU ARE MY MEMORIES OF YOU
holding my hand.
I introduce the human
with this cut-out figure of my mind.
Y
O
U
are so brutal,
my stomach shudders.

A little boy
is happy with his Mama's
SONG
about three pigs and a bear escaping
to the hills.
It is always the same
grim happy ending.
The wet eucalyptus trunk creaking,
is as liberated
as a brown moth
in the deck light.
I SMILE
AT STARS
above
ripples
of the nearby Bay
and
fill
with their ebullience and comity.

MEPHISTO 10

MOUNTAINS OF MATTER

MADE OF STARS,

and
scent of crushed
GERANIUM LEAVES,
in "the everlasting universe of things"
roll through Shelley's mind
and drop countless kalpas
to the snow leopard fur
behind
THE BABY'S EYES.
A hiss of anger turns to a growl
and a kiss,
like the seasons
and red-purple petals
banked against curbs.

Gold-tipped cigarettes,
veiling dark lashes, hard winter pears,
these have never been
MORE CLEAR.

Psyche, nous, pneumas, whatever,
has not only come together
extending realms
and removing the old bounds
they
also unfold
outwards.

MEPHISTO 11

BRAVE, FEARFUL, SCARED TO DEATH
by the boredom. A fat gray kitten rolls
on his back sinking baby claws
(clean thin baby claws)
into the pink flesh.

Now I am the eagle of my face
with white crest reaching my shoulders
and the deep eyes that never
change, never change
from the outward. (A steppe
of valleys and wrinkles.)

As another god
I threw the sight of one eye
to the salmon leaping
in the pool. — Thought and memory
fly to me on their black wings.

ALWAYS
BEING
BORN
smells like pepper.

Nothing fears me when I smile
at the miner's lettuce on the bank.

And the odor!
The other odor! — As kind
as the insides of your knees.

MEPHISTO 12

"MIND" MEANS NOTHING BUT CONSCIOUSNESS —
a rock has it and a toadstool
and a field of particles in a complex protein.
It is as myriad as a lazing pollywog
and an imagined cluster of dimensions.
Nimbleness is the strength of a killer whale
with a screaming sea lion in her mouth
and white teeth((((,
AND
THIS
SPRING
is as delicate as a view
of your calf when your robe
falls open while you stand at the sink.
Proportionless-ness holds
none of this
together.
"Liberation" is a pitch for
who we are
and
much
of
it
lacks
the sizeless humor
of poetry
and
truth.

MEPHISTO 13

THIS IS ALL A STRING OF PEARLS
with reflections of reflections in the opulent
glimmering surface of endless flaws.
NATURE
(IS)
HIDING.

The green house front and the smell
of Dogen Creek in the rain,
with the budding buckeyes
ARE HEAVEN
for juncos flitting
in the wet undergrowth.

Train calls weave
through Vivaldi concerts
in the downpour.
Overstretched pink earthworms
come out and lie
on the drenched
TARMAC.

Panta rei is one idea,
and a death and a chickpea
have the same weight
on
no
scales.

MEPHISTO 14

YOU ARE
everyone
BUT
I am nobody.
Nobody is large and powerful
as the flecks and colonies
of lives — sessile,
burning and whirling —
on the fronds of brown kelp
in the seawater.
Nudged by stars they
are
B
E
I
N
G
LIGHT.

Black pepper on the bowl
of cottage cheese
and rain clouds
are ding an sich.
Child voices on the street
speak of blackberries
and electronic heroes
clambering out of their boxes.

(Time for rest.)

MEPHISTO 15

WATER BOILS IN THE BIG COPPER TUB. White sheets
will be dipped in the bluing. Wrung out in the wringer
and then hung up to dry. THE SUBSTRATE IS SO VIBRANT,
my Grandmother shimmers in it, LOOKING
THROUGH (HER) THICK GOGGLE GLASSES
with oversize brown eyes. "How can you be
so calm on your outside,
Michael?
I know how much you are feeling inside."

— I imagine hollow logs where raccoons might sleep
and watch for white footed deer mice.

Barrage balloons lifting cables
protect the B17 Flying Fortress factories.
ONE
ex
q
u
i
s
i
t
e
garter snake gleams in sun
on a junk tire
in the wrack of the glade.

A few fiddle neck ferns.

MEPHISTO 16

INSIDE OUT LIKE A PROTEIN the owl hoots.
The hurt locker. Easy virtue
with mist of pink smoke.

I

A
M
THE
GRAIL.
My wrist measures all.
The chest of a beast speaks in the rain.
The brown hills are green
and one golden violet
lifts up in the field.
Twin Peaks are the city's nipples
as white mohair fogs slips
over and around them,
beautiful as tropes of Heraclitus' voice,
or a big game hunter watching the stars
and keeping the Moon's changes
on a chunk of ivory in the firelight
of burning bones and fat.
A
L
W
A
Y
S
ME.

BIG CLEAR LAUGHS ARE THE BEST
and deep seeing eyes
and a loud exuberant cry of "YES!"
— DETERMINING THE PATHS OF SPIRIT
is done with THOSE tools,
and imagined death runs away
on tiptoe
while the white dog
B
A
R
K
S
and blinks her beautiful lids.
Beginningless heavens of moments
hold us in their arms
and are the MATRIX
of a dark forest sheltering a glade
of liberation.

Everything is less than a child's toothache
on a bright day.

The hailstorm is shaped
like an old haystack
with white-silver pellets
rattling the patio.

MEPHISTO 18

IN THE PLANE ROAR
IS A FORGOTTEN MOMENT
and another, and another…
and another…
spreading in the numb ears and eyes
like the atoms of Democritus
and the intense passions of fruit flies.
Dumb, unknowable,
springing directly and elegantly
from hidden Nature
in unexpected shapes
UNLESS
I remember
that we also are bodies
with excrescences and soft pits and love
and melodious voices and buzzes,
making our own dear odes
to fallen daisies
and
inseparable
from the unsounding roar
OF GALAXIES
and nutrients moving to the doors
of root tendrils.

MEPHISTO 19

"IT DON'T MAKE SENSE BUT IT'S IMMENSE."

R
O
A
R
of beings and engines
in the child's heart and shoulders
expands to make flesh that we live in.
It's a nitrous oxide high in the dentist chair
remembered in universal directions and realms.

A
N
D

I
am the center
as is the petal floating and falling and spinning
in morning light
and the jaguar speedster on 101.
(Tough black plastic rubber over miles of concrete.)
Now tree frogs sing in the gloaming.
You park in the wealthy neighborhood
with ponds, stately dark trees, and a gate.
I touch your leg
under wool slacks.

The whirligig is calm
around us.

MEPHISTO 20

SOFT TOES CURL ON THE FLOOR. PRIMATE STYLE
with gleam of varnished wood beneath them.
The garden does not sleep at night.
THE POWERFUL KNOWLEDGE
is all around. The cortex, is the shape
of a self-curled and wide-spread butterfly;
wings open in scents and all probable
stream bottoms
finding stars, blotches of odor
and pulses of organs
in unlighted dimensions
and awakening chakras.
IT
IS
CORE ESSENCE
of nothingness.
Like the twitch of a zebra's haunch
in the herd by the game lodge
at the lip of the crater.

You know me by my
white-haired adventures
on the cliff edge.

MEPHISTO 21

THE CLOUD THAT RAPHAEL FOUND is the rules of freedom.
  Dark green shamrocks growing in a bowl where
dead friends live in dreams. (Talk of consciousness
        is little compared to this.) They
    are often younger and half someone else.
    It's you, only you, who is solid,
    solid and deep and lynx-eyed
        in the third day of Spring.
      New grass waves high,
    swept in the small breeze of Zephyrus.
      The leaves of suncups
        force back their neighbors
      and their yellow eyes and mouths
        embrace the sky.
    By the johnny jump ups and the vetch
    pale purple mallow lifts high above them.
            BEGIN AGAIN
          Whitehead:
        the new year on the day of Gabriel.
          is
            a
          part
        of no process.

MEPHISTO 22

HEART-ACHE NEWS WITH THE TORTURED FACES
and grim boredom verging on insolence
and a rifle slung over the shoulders
is passé in the blast of entertainment
from walls, machines, and surfaces.
DRONE PLANES FLASH
as seasons disrupt.
BLUE FIN TUNA AND RED SALMON,
sliced raw on a white plate
face each other
while engines carve and fly
through walls
of cold-smelling coal.
The story of inescapable
rise to betterment
is the march of all beings
AND NON-BEINGS

E
N
CAPSULED
in the yellow sun and lengthening shadow

— it's one face) unable to prevaricate
or pretend to be anything other than naked imagination.

MEPHISTO 23

FACES
TWISTED
in pain
(from the old times when love hurt
so much that it was spotlights
filled with legs and mouths
writhing)
are
a column of paramecia
and protista hula-dancing
OUR
LIVES.
But you are the flesh
that shapes my Heart.
Our dyad is fingers touching,
in dark morning, under sheets
with robins wakening.

We believe the last dance of Merce Cunningham
is a face of William Blake.

It is time to bend, naked,
and lift the helpless silverfish
from the maelstrom of the shower
and put her
in a gentle place.

Truth and Beauty have no age, ending, or beginning,
they are imaginary wings on our foreheads.

MEPHISTO 24

MIRO KNOWS IT IS ALL PLAY AND POLLOCK UNDER
STANDS
the unconscious power.
CONSCIOUSNESS
RISES
in a cluster of flowers.
EACH SCALLOPED WHITE PETAL
with a border
of
venetian
purple
is bright as a polar bear's eyes.
At the center of each bloom
are four golden-yellow balls.
By the trailer on the hill
horses eye the feathered chicks
that scatter under their feet
and the boson becomes a comic book.
NAKED BEAUTY
and realm heaped upon realm
are
much
like this
but more laughable and more serious.

MEPHISTO 25

I AM THE ONE IT ALL HAPPENS AROUND:
coal, star clusters, time/space, and the hungers of landlords.
A skunk, in the yard at the edge of the stones, is watched closely
by the calico cat

IT

IS

SO

SERIOUS

and real
like the scar on Odysseus' knee.
THERE ARE NO BEGINNINGS OR BOUNDARIES
and protein continues on in full belief,
unfolding
growing richer
and feasting on the leakage
of metaphors
while the deep-purple blue dicks
stand up in the rain.

MEPHISTO 26

LIKE A MOTH OR A HUMMINGBIRD TURNED INSIDE
OUT
in the lightning once seen at the tips of the wings
and the smell of an egg salad sandwich
in the darkness where nothing sings
but the tuning of neurons.

This is all tremor in the rattle of film
and cartoons
and snow sparkling Rockies before
dharmadatu is here for the touching.
Velveteen voice on the eardrums,
touch of cold plastic coffee cup to the fingers.
No cloud nebula, Rothko,
blooming fuchsia, scent of Guerlain
is a ten-trillionth as lovely
as you, naked, riding me,
laughing, dancing,
and your blond hair
swirling about
as
you
laugh.

A toddler, screaming, writhing, in endless pain
of his new tooth.

Vanity, protein, and warm sunlight
are stones on the littoral —
are all dharmadatu.

THIS
CITY
OF
MY HEART
was once innocent as a baby and we
grew up in it. Pictures of greed
SLIDE
NOW
on walls looking for faces
to grow onto (upon) behind the wheels of cars.
Vaults of dainties in hotel rooms
vend hunger for dollars
to buy lost love as it reflects
glories of stars on the river.

What fortune to be here,
we'll take off on vast wings
POWERED
by inspiration
and land again in the worlds
from which we seemed to arise
as real
as lions in a field of high grass
AND A CARTOON MOUSE HEAD
on a pale green, short sleeve tee shirt.
We flirt with
insubstantiality.

MEPHISTO 28

THE THORNS IN MY FINGER MAKE STARS.
The blackberry is sweet and black
and red and bitter.
Now consciousness slides from one echo
of the endocranial bone house
TO THE OTHER.
It is not neurons or biochemicals!

Butterfly means psyche,
and now it opens out, stretches,
into the breeze in the attic
when windows rattle
— and in another direction
into the coal pit of odors.
It looks down and smiles
at the drop of blood
on the meaty, intelligent
KNOWING PAD
of this finger

and I disappear into stuff
like Nature hiding herself
and reappear

WITH A GRIN.

AND I OUGHT

to be scared as my skin wrinkles. The boy dreams
of grandpa. As the moon gets huger there are streams
stretching into shadows of memories
of red flowers on the cliffs and faces around me.
On the paths high above there are old friends
with clouded faces. But the blur
is a mirror of my own incompleteness.
Racing cars seen on shattered obsidian

SURFACES

are

like

that

and the eyes of wolves looking
upward through gravel.
Here and now I want you to be as we always are
in this flickering moment.

You and I are a candle
on this dark, scarred end-table.
EVERYTHING IS BEAUTY

EVEN THE LOSS

of dear ones and crashed hopes
making

a

bonfire.

MEPHISTO 30

NOW

THERE

ARE

LIONS

roaring clouds of nothingness
comprised of billions of worlds and pools

a

b

o

v

e

BOSTON

AGAIN.

Wild red columbines are drawn into the breeze of passing bikers
and this can be swimming and floating
in high powerful green waves
at the littoral of Tulum temple
not far from the jaguarundi stepping
with dainty feet in the forest.

ALL CONSTRUCTED WORLDS MUST BE SO
to carry the weight and the emptiness of the real one.
And I love to be in our cave with you
among sculptures of horse heads and chickadees
feeding their young in the eves.
The licorice fern will let its root
go deeper in wet soil
by the eucalyptus stump.

MEPHISTO 31

YOU ARE MY MEMORIES OF YOU
holding my hand
I
WANT
TO
GO
everywhere with you infinite times.
These are the moments of my flesh
reaching ceaselessly, touching fingers
in the lynxlight of your eyes
twined with my boyish gloom.
We only go where there are beaches and endless light
and darkness with constellations
and rattling and creaking of taxis
from the airport to this hummingbird zen hut.
THIS
IS
US.

THIS IS SAMSARA

right on the edge
of breaking though
to nothingness
that is far less than smoke.

EAGLES SEEN ON ACID are the rules
that are broken in old poetry. The fierce eyes,
the naying hand of the boy
are the imagination
SHAPING
INSPIRATION
from an edge beyond senses
and made wholly
of reflections in qualia.
NOT true!
Translucent red-orange of the indian paintbrush,
smell of gasoline at the pumps,
are not much
and the trainwreck of tradition
is seen in the breath
OF OLD MASTERS.

ALL
WAYS

THE
CENTER
is a naked statue
of gold and ivory.

RICE PADDIES ARE LOADED WITH SOULS
and molecules of agent orange
in suspension among children of mosquitoes
whipping their tails for air.
BUT
THIS
PARADISE
is under the silver unblushing star of Venus
against perfect lavender blue
and the silhouette of the mountain.
In this spot a calico cat
stared upward into morning.
Every moment and whisker
is startled
into
totality of her being
EVERYWHERE.   (small case
There is no desuetude,
ALL
IS
LIFE
and our beloved friends,
and cadre, debouch

right here
of all
places.

MEPHISTO 34

"GIVE WAY OR BE SMITTEN INTO NOTHINGNESS
and everlasting night" but I am here already
and the tips of my fingers set free light
— here in meatspirit, lying my head on dense moss,
moss on the stones of the canyon.

GOODBYE. HELLO.

Farewell friend.

We are together in the movies and watching
THE SCENE.
We are here in the media with simpers and spleen.
OUR REAL LEGS
of skin, hair, and muscle
are those we stand
up ON.

Trillions of moments
are not the occasion
of
a
momentary life.

Friendship and dyads are free
in these strata.
I am utterly partially
FREE
where hummingbirds flash
over moonlit snow.

GOING
the way of all flesh
caught in the hum of the furnace
as the small bell rings:
Dogen says of Deep Ocean Samhadi,
"disappearance is neither sequential or aligned,"
not even the fall of incense flakes
into sparkling red charcoal,
or mingled matter and nothingness
poured from cup to cup
is
independent.

BUT
ALL IS
SO GOOD,
the odor of the fat pink rose
pressed to the face
before
the burial
of ashes

in the black vase
in the cedar box.
FEAR
and
LOVE
are PEARL moments.
Moments reflecting.

Swing low sweet chariot.

NOW I SMELL MY GRANDMA AS SHE LOOKS
through the bay windows to the ocean:
spice cake, bakers chocolate,
ham hocks, lima beans and disinfectant.
Raspberries in the garden
are fruits of her hands and sunlight and gases.
Paraffin-topped jars of jam fill the closets.
Paradise is the homeland
of the black-whiskered baby catfish
swimming above their shadows
on the velvet bottomed
edge of the lake. I lie on crusty mud
reaching
for
them.

Green and mauve sea anemones
and barnacles on the piles
A
R
E
old.
But Dear Being you are the oldest soul.
Naked, all things comprise you:
the mountains, the beaches, a dog
barking on the ridge.
In your presence: I am.
Redtail hawks hover over us.
Moments hold us in their arms
like kittens awakening.

MEPHISTO 37

SUNSET COLORS OF APRICOT AND LAYERS OF BLACK
over the ocean and moment-memories of round hills
with a lion roar and exhaust from the car
running a-mix with the first buckeye butterfly
OF SUMMER
and boughs

OF PURPLE LILAC.

At
last,
like always, I am a MAMMAL,

man-mammal being time,
being true,
your
LOVER,

as Ashvagosha loves and Lord Byron does,
and the intoxicated water fly mad for stuff
of being. The protozoan, garnet,
and stardust are our teeth and lips
clinging lightly to the edge.
AND
MY
EYES
and my fingertips
are
yours.
No difference.

No difference in the opal sky and the mountain.

SOME FRINGES

some are buckskin
some are tangled
some are silk and beach wrack

THE MYSTERY OF THE HUNT
for Tom and Leslie

1

LOOKING UP,
the gopher sees
sunlight
reflecting
in the bobcat's
eyes

2

A CLAW-FRINGED PAW
h
a
n
g
s
exquisitely still,
no twitch,

WHAM
!

MY
MOSS
HEAD
(tiny red
maple
leaves,
lichens)

makes
light

MY FACE IS
A ROCK
LUMPED BY
MOSS
crusty lichens

small red leaves

NEW MOON   ((BLACK!))
STAR CLOUDS

HALOES

Flashlight reflects
in two small eyes

gut-
T
W
I
S
T
I
N
G
beauty of science
journals
on shiny
pages

THE HAPPY
WHITE DOG
with black eyes
rolls
in deer shit

Wave-crash
nearby

SKY MEAT

For George Brooks

SKY MEAT
PEEPING THROUGH
BLUE, GRAY, BLACK

at
wave-crash

Lush ripples

WAVE BOOMS
BOOM
BOOM
on
sheer
cliff crumble

(Silver
ripples
float
kelp snakes)

WET
BEACH ROCK
JEWELS
fall
apart
in
crash

SKINNY
SURF
GREBES
dive

I AM THE FIRELIGHT,
THE MIRROR.
In
between
are beach flies

TWO HAIKU

NOVEMBER CRICKETS
chirping in the wind:
deer turds
black
on
the
ground

ROSE GLOW
on the twilight wall
and cat on the purple
tee
shirt

REFINED AS A WILD
BLACKBERRY
I am
this
old face
and
HANDPRINT

WHITE CHRYSANTHEMUM
and ripening persimmon,
in
winter
sun

— YULE LOG SHINING
FLICKER
ING

on tv:

(real

rain

on the roof

DRESSED
in
SKIN
and
soul-making:
many
beings
on wave-wet rocks

GOBBETS OF FOAM RUSH
through the beach rock's shadow,
like sandpipers

DARKNESS —

HAIL FLURRY
on the window!
THUMP
(to floor)
goes the cat

In sun,
ODD BROWN
sow bug people
H
I
D
E
OUT
in my tin mailbox

HAIKU-LIKE
the
dried
up
wild
rose
trembles

FOR GARY

1

LOOK, SCARLET COLUMBINE,
April sun!
Honeysuckle's
almost here!

2

OPEN UP, REDWOOD ROSE,
blackberry blossoms
are arriving

3

BLUE-EYED GRASS,
Indian paintbrush
— great
companions!

GRAY SILVERFISH BLUR
streaks
across sheet,
under pillow:
I grab!

THIS TINY, CURLED
(GRAY-BLACK) PILL BUG
is

consciousness

FEATHER-SCATTER BOUQUET
— death by fox!
Unlucky young
rooster
prince!

THE WING-FACE OF THE LITTLE
BROWN MOTH
looks up
desperately

IN SUMMER SOLSTICE
twilight shine,
robins stride
almost
touching
wings

DEEP IN THE PINK FLOWER'S
yellow center,
my face

My face?

LOVELY ELONGATED LOPING
COYOTE
speeding
to the beach dunes

BULGING HUMMINGBIRD EYES

Pale lavender
flower

!!!

OH

Sacred mint!

(*Salvia divinorum*)

MID-AIR — THE SILVER-GREEN
HUMMINGBIRD
wrestles
purple flowers

THE NEARBY LEMON BLOSSOM
SCENT
wrestles
the
hummingbird's mind

RAGGED WINGED YOUNG BUTTERFLY
— hungers still not
satisfied?

FREE AS A TIGER TABBY
in her striped bars
of purring

SOMETIMES THE CAT PURRING
smells like cedar
with blue
eyes
staring

PERFECT BLACK SHADOWS

Tiny catfish

whiskers
moving
on
the
silt

ROSE BREATHS

after sitting on the black cushion

MONKEY MIND AND ROSE-BREATHING
are a face of consciousness
struggling to be plain meatly
and perfect
as a bouquet of rosemary,
chrysanthemums, and a daisy
— in hell worlds striving
to be heavens

2

BETWEEN ROSE BREATHS I AM FLOODED
with love and desire for your flesh.
THIS IS MY DHARMA:
you beside me quietly
in blue robe
and bare toes.
I WILL GIVE MONEY
deep from my heart
to save whales
and seals and keep blood
from the ocean

SLEEP SWELLING WITH ROSE BREATHS
— A RUMPUS OF WAVES —
over and under — quiet and huge.
The ACHE in the back
BEING THE CALL TO DEEP EYES
looking everywhere. THE SCRIM
is what we live by, secretly
KNOWING
WE ALWAYS KNOW
in half-sleep and rose-breathing

4

RIDING ROSE BREATHS, CLOUD-WALKING
through oceans between cliffs
part-dreaming seeking for unadorned center.
ALWAYS THERE.
HERE I AM IN THE CENTER
of this ride. Seeking for stillness
and
secretly
enjoying the thrill.
BEING SOLID IN NOTHINGNESS
steady, always almost steady, on the shaky edge
BUT
NOT
solid

5

SMELL OF FRUIT COMPOTE — COFFEE-MAKING —
BRIGHT BLUE
OF LARKSPUR
floating in front of my mind —
PAUSES, PAUSES
between rose breaths and the noses
of counting. A GOOD PRIDE
LIFTING, LIFTING UP FROM PELVIS.
Struggling with the dream
bumpings of numbers. This
IS ALWAYS THE WAY
shaking off inhibition, shedding the lace.

6

ROSE BREATH HARMLESS AS LIFE
AND DEATH — and one clear blue eye
staring at the sound of the cat eating
CRUNCHY FOOD. AND THE HIGH WALLS
around.
A turbulent ride through the smoothness.
Meat here pretending to be meat
and spirit and hiding
from luminous non-meaning
of goodbye

to

the

trip

THE SEA OF ROSE BREATHS
IS CALM and imagined
by the sun of flowers
— in light on hilltops.
Death drops
behind and weights
like froth at the morning crests
where lives of silverfish
and planets float in
wavering almost clear waves
with chips of shells
and an uplift
and a down

ROSE BREATHS — ROSE BREATHS SPENT
— wasted maybe! No! HOW! Day-
dreaming of a poet friend.
Adventurer and defender of whale
CONSCIOUSNESS.
S
L
I
D
E
S.
FLOATING AMONG
ROSE
BREATHS.
Tide — a surge carrying
transparent chips of memory and protein

9

ROSE SCENT BUD BREATHS INCENSE
BREATH   SHALLOW   DEEP
incense of mum and rosemary plucked
as a string is. A RAVEN QUARKS
FLYING LOW TO "HELLO," SLIPS
into rose breathing as even
a flock of band-tail pigeons breathe
in the beginningless change
BUT
NOT
not ever flowing just a sleeping dream
and dreaming wide awake

PEEKING AT SCARLET, PINK, WHITE,
green fronds. TIGER ROSE BREATHS.
SNOW LION FACE. Big consciousness
in bodhisattva words. Worlds. Cloud gone
whole sky open in closed eyes
B
L
E
E
D
ING
ROSE BREATHS VISAGE
of Manjusri's swinging flame sword
sliding open barricades between
realms. Just breathing. Just tuning
like Bach and mystic avalanche trumpets
of tattered silk silence,
absolutely still and empty of a goal

11

MONKEY MIND IS PEACE IN ROSE BREATHS
when Stan Brakhage is
wandering with the bears and the eagles
eating a cave into the STRANDED WHALE body.
JUST
SMOOTH
PEACE AS THERE IS
always a thing afloat
like a sailing ship in the beginningless.
— DEAD FRIENDS NEVER LEAVING
their moments
float everywhere in their sizeless moments

12

EVEN IN THE SMELL OF THE NEW
RED SHOULDER SHAWL, QUIETUDE
breaks up into emptinesses filled
with absence of ROSE BREATHS — and
the old truck clambers
up the hill outside.
This may be the presence of what needs to be
for the long muscle in pain
in my back, while Kwannon
is occupied with mice, whales,
jerusalem crickets, and the splintering
spine of a distant friend

13

Rohatsu, for Leslie

CONSCIOUSNESS IS NOTHING NOT
EVEN NOTHINGNESS
where bears lumber out from the underbelly
of the whale. — Filled with the cave
that might or might not be flesh

o

n

l

y

ROSE BREATHS ARE SOLID
with uplift and download
OF DELUSION
and smell of clean rot
from
nada beaches
and green and pink breakers of high walls
imagining along (inwards and outwards)

14

ROSE BLACK OUT OF NOTHING ROSE
in space between lifting petals
of breathing or not.
And minuscule red mites
marching, climbing, trailing
on hydrangea. Just past the corner
of consciousness. BIG BREATHE.
BREATHING
of
nothing.
No Bo Tree no teeth no nothing
but hope of hands and arms of compassion

DARK BREATHING ROSE BREATHES GRAY
where candle flame enters. And
INCENSE in calm turgid wavers
raise and grow as life
and death doorway is more
than spirit. More than intelligence
it is always THIS WAY
as it shall be now. CLOSE
to solstice are waves,
flat and calm
and the tremor uplifts,
misreads itself as the frisson
of everything as emptiness
under emptiness

16

RIDING UPWARD AND DOWNWARD
OUT OF AMARYLLIS GRAVEL,
ROSE
B
R
E
A
T
H
S
gray as dead carnations. INCARNATE
IN BREATH and nonbeing of nonbeing
like the sailing ship
AT THE BEAR'S FEAST,
the light tread of the mind-foot
and heart-paw stands with
our tides.
And we float on. THUS
is nothingness.
No more please

ROSE BREATHS BREATHING REAL
of the fragrant pink
rosebud among scarlet chrysanthemums
in candle glow and green incense
with fog cloud behind at deck windows
— and the cat speaks
clearly and modestly,
matter-of-factly, of nearness
OF HER DEATH
and her old age of cat life,
and of mine in the sadness
of being a big monkey

BEING

THUMBPRINT

for Bruce Conner

CLIFFS OF BURSTS!!!   Raging — stretching out in branches

      SUN-STRUCK   NOVEMBER   EAST WIND,
      CREAKING EUCALYPTUS BOUGHS.
        And the black cat GRINS
        under the red salvia bush.

      I AM   FOREVER   BLISSED

        forever blessed

      MY EYES BLINK CLOSED
      and then open.

      The war AGAINST SPIRIT
                 AND NATURE
      is over my left shoulder.
      Where it
      ALWAYS IS.

      Aunt Fanny, in the bedroom,
   peers clear-eyed from an unlined face
   in a gold frame by the bead-clustered
Masai bracelet that smells of Kenyan cow shit.

            *

        • •

      THIS INSTANT,   standing on its paws,
        reaches endlessly
        through stars

and ripples, and froths out on beaches,
where elephant seals with bleeding necks
                    TRUMPET
            in the sunset
        and tiny isopods
                    nestle between pebbles
            shivering with sheer joy of power
        and nothingness

SESTINA FOR AMY

1

I SLEEP WITH YOU but never enough, LOVER,
for your ever-reshaping body is delight
SOFT WARM PRECIOUS SWEET   TENDER
in fragments   we awake and laugh
and there are RAVEN QUARKS AND TRUCKS
WE ARE ALWAYS by a MOUNTAIN.

2

WAR-SCREAMS, screened by the tar mountain
can't stop me being your lover
our spirits have the power of silver trucks
and from this truth we wring delight
which can fly about like a child's laugh.
No matter how brutal is the dharmadhatu,
                                IT'S TENDER.

3

EDGES of forest and moss are tender
and stress and despair will shape a mountain;
there is loveliness in the damage of LAUGHS.
YOU AND I   feel the touch   of a lover
and each star bank is a synapse of delight,
as rain and flowers are moved by trucks.

4

REST   will never be delivered by trucks
and that cruelty lets us know to be tender.
SEEING HUMMINGBIRDS flash through pain is delight,
they are not blocked by a highway or mountain;

the cloud of dark blue rain is a lover
and the dry time to come is a laugh.

5

Your heels move in morning with a laugh
when we think about sun and trucks.
The green odor of basil reminds us of a lover
even tire tracks on a worm are tender
when the huge cruelty of a mountain
is a mask for the physique of delight.

6

WE KNOW   the PHYSICS of delight
is dressed with scowls and we laugh
with compassion for universe and mountain,
tiniest capillaries entunnel living trucks.
Even the most hideous background is tender
when I wake for a moment with YOU my
                                        LOVER.

envoy

DELIGHT is the least costly gift in the truck
and the laugh of the cliff is tender;
this mountain and bouquet reveal that I am your lover.

UNDERTOW
for Dave Haselwood

IMAGINE THE UNDERTOW OF SAMSARA TO BE A WAVE
LOOMING OVER US — WE TINY PARTICLES OF BIO
STUFF
IN THE UNDERSURGE — CHUNKS OF
PHYTOPLANKTON,
CLAM LARVAE, PHARMACEUTICAL MOLECULES,
SMASHED DNA, MOTHER KILLERS,
sizeless dimensions of greed,
ineffable swirls of psychic density,
hormone-ribbon drifts,
colliding archipelagoes of lies, KILLER MOTHERS,
solid nothingnesses in endless sensory modes
of taste and fright — stridings of nonexistence
for blood power and Godiva fudge creams
or
a sip of drinkable water.

BROKEN BACTERIA CONJUGATING,
presidential power fantasies,
unknown plasmas of miniature hell worlds
— frighten us out of consciousness
TO
KNOW
OURSELVES
only
AS
RIFFLE BITS.

BUT
A
COUNTERFORCE
is

the invention of love and building of soul
and not to be protections or armor
BUT to be REAL BEING BEING REAL.

Not love as a dribbling idea we tap into,
as the disruption rushes
in its hypermetabolic onslaught
but
to build love so that we may have brief presence
in the ceaseless samsaric undertow

and truly touch a wrist
or cheek

FOR INGRID ROSEN HARBAUM

IT IS NOT MODULAR HUNKS OF A NEURON
MEAT ORGAN, and neural circuitry,
but more and infinitely less — like the blissful face,
smooth and unlined, perfect in skills
and black whiskers of an extinct fox,
or the gentle eyes of a marsupial wolf.
Something is alive and transparent
in the Hadal deep ocean
or on a sun's surface
singing lover to lover
in fire storms
EXACTLY THE SAME FOR US!
AND THAT'S THE TOP LAYER
of the interweaving of matters
and non-matters
BURIED IN CONSCIOUSNESS
way down in the star banks
that hang like mud at the edge of a puddle
for the lengthening red and brown
earthworm under the forest of gold-sided ferns.
Like that.   That is it.

SO YEAH

for Reinhard Harbaum

SO YEAH,

DO LOVE LIFE AS LIFE LOVES

BUT NOT

the social training

Drop it. Forget it!   Inventing the shape,

let loose of duty, like a spirit floating

and ride waves of spontaneous good feeling.

That's heaven's coast with the smiling cat looking at me,

right back in my mammal eye.

EVERYWHERE IN THE BILLIONTH

OF THE MOMENT

the mountain *lours* above, and Dogen Creek

floods for the pleasure of the listening deer.

We

CALL THAT HOME.

— It's right under the glimmering salmon sunset,

also on a distant beach gathering flat rock

— sometimes even the rubbery smell of the freeway

Rimbaud wanted to achieve this.

Whitman's boots walked over the top of it.

The Pacific Ocean, bringing

Asian voices, saved us from centuries

of rusty cinders

SKAAGI THE SALMON

for Jerome Rothenberg

WITHIN THE FACES OF HUNGER ARE FACES
OF HUNGER (within faces of hungers)
and tadpoles and teeth surging
towards souls they devour. DEVOUR
AND NIBBLE
and chase laughing through waves
INTO THE AIR FOLLOWING THE GREAT FACE
of jaws and smiles and growls
ON THE POWERFUL TAIL. Fins
of lives turn to sunset over
misty islands
AS WE SPEED TO THE FEATURES
of love always alight as we create delight
ahead. (Crumbs of meat in the wake.)
THIS IS THE TRUTH
OF THE HALF-LIE
speedily moving with no splashes.
Even the adipose fin has an eye.
NO REASON TO CRY
F
O
R

LIFE

it is coming and going.

— *after a Haida drawing*
by Bill Reid

MOUNT TAMALPAIS

for Etel Adnan

"COLOR IS THE SIGN OF THE EXISTENCE OF LIFE"
it lives in the perception of waves of numinous-
ness
— no
V
O
Y
A
N
C
E,
no Novalis, no Etel, no cliffs, no sky
without art coming out of the black. We dye,
with stone-pale sumi, and let lie
the inert eye and numb fingertip.
The blackberry, purple iris, quark of the raven
are endlessly craved to birth our souls.
"The wild garden becomes a moving patch
on the floor of the forest."
Torments dream us as we answer with bliss
made of flames and fires and blind tsunamis,
making soul-science and meat spirit
as they fill the coldness and emptiness with glamour.
We are the mindless hoo-ing on the streets
and the paradisos of bacteria
as we sleep listening to foxes
when they bark by their dens
at the top of the ridge,
under the forest above the smile of the surf,
on a slope-side near the top
of the mountain.

FOR PHILIP LAMANTIA

WHAT ROTTINGS WE BLASTED OUT
                    AND GLEAMED TOGETHER
        to flaunt and nourish separate paradisos!
    — Yours in the sky, high on prayers and opium.
            — Mine in meat aches and rose glow
                    — meshing
                as they loomed apart.
        — We abjured half-hidings and ego tricks.
— THE WARS WERE OURS
                    IN BLACKEST RADIOACTIVE SHINE
        also the peace we won and successes of our torture
                                and the lips of pain
    for particles of liberty that sometimes stuck together.

    Heavy on consciousness and easy on sense,

                EASY ON SENSE,

                in overlapping realms
                of being-time

                        it
                    will

            NEVER BE OVER!

FOR GEORGE BROOKS

DEEP SCARS ON THE FACE ARE EACH
a love conquest — the shallow ones
ARE GOOD FAILURES.
WALKING ON THE FOOTPRINTS OF SAND
between willows, the rioting SURF
rises to the feet of pelicans.
MORTALITY IS BEAUTY / THE BEAST SPIRIT
l
i
v
e
s
and Pollock roils his "Elegant Lady"
split in demeanor
and laughing at cells SCULPTING
SELVES.
I replace the beak and skull in the thin reeds.
Here is indian paintbrush
and bee bush.

Last night's moonlight spreads here.

FOR GARRETT AND SUZANNE

BIG DUMB ANIMAL STATES
PULSE OF DELUSION

MINEFIELDS OF ILLUSION

the blue, green, ochre, and raspberry
of all we know

loves and births
in breasts of touch
and reflections of fire in snow

we are

POETS

S
M
I
L
I
N
G

in the trembling roar

POLLOCK'S *ECHO*
   for George Stanley

THE SUN COMES AND GOES WITH THE ECHO, THE
ROSES,
AND THE BIG FLAT EAR,
IN THE CAVE OF DARKNESS.
IT IS PERSONS AND A FALCON FACE
HELD IN THE BEAUTY-RAW-PERFECTION
OF THEIR NON-MOVEMENT, NON-SWIRLING,
IN A WHIRL OF NUTMEGS AND FOOTPRINTS,
AND MOTHER MOTHS BEING MOTHERS OF ALL
WITH THE MAPS ON THEIR WINGS THROWN OVER
WHERE A WALL WOULD BE

if this were not Pollock's consciousness
as it ages and steeps clear in alcohol and the

slithering
away of earlier torments
I
N
T
O
this clear bright
living
that I see myself by

— *Echo* hangs on a surface or maybe
is alive in space

— *Vancouver*

ANACREON'S CUPID

CUPID DOES NOT SEE A BEE
snoozing among roses
and is wounded in his hand,
on the finger.
He screams and runs and flies
to the voluptuous Venus, shrieking.
"I am slain, Mama! Mama, I die!
I am pierced by a little winged snake
that the farmer calls a bee."
And she answers, "If the bee sting pains you,
how much do they suffer, Cupid,
whom you strike with your arrows."

ANACREON MEETING CUPID

THE BOY BENDING BESIDE ME PICKING ROSES
slips up and shows a flash
OF HIS WINGS
though he tries to hide them.
"RUN," I think, seeing his little bow
and crystal arrows.
Fleeing, I feel his shaft
pierce my back
AND
I
SEE
the point
pop from my chest
dripping heart's blood.
Now I laugh and weep.
I do not cut my hair
and my white beard scratches
the wine cup.

SMALL ODE ON THE NEED TO DRINK

(after Anacreon)

The Cherubim
know most. The Daimons love most.
I'M A SERAPH
— let me learn eternally
the shape of the lovely bosom.

— And drink champagne
and write odes
to Drambuie
among the stars.
The black sea drinks and the clouds drink her.
Then why, amongst all creatures,
must not I?

A BLUE ROSE

(after Anacreon)

VENUS, HERMES, DIANA: *LOOK, A BLUE ROSE!*
THE EAGLE HAS ENTERED
my senses
and I have become divine! Even
fearing death — or pretending that I do —
when now I know, this being,
this reality, THIS DARK THUNDER-PINK,
THIS ROAR, this smelling of roses,
and reaching to touch petals,
is here.
And needs no duration,
breathing you.

EPITHALAMION

for Nic and Bonnie Saunders

THERE WILL BE BLUE VELVET, SHARP TEETH,
AND PURRING OF LIONS IN NEW ALBION.

LIVES IN THE MORNING AIR.
AUGUST CLEAR AND EVENING FAIR.

This moment is your body
and you are everywhere
— in those who came before
and those who follow after.

SMILES OF ROSES IN THE AIR,
WREATHS OF IVY AND BOSKY SCENT
— they are yours joined together.

Music in the air and cake
and nuptial bed to welcome both
into one.
One dyad — but more yet
to arrive with bare feet
on the shining stair.
This day sings many wings
to welcome bride
and groom to spread their selves
and end all secrecy with eros song
and grinning future.

You are in Eternity,
and chasing beauty.

FOR TOM

"TRANSIENCY LIKE THE SHAPE OF WATER
is permanent"
— like stardust and arms of Kwannon.
We are quiet as whales and mice and before long
morning and flower-breath
begin again,
for in the depths everything is known
and a rock may have courage
and warm blood,
and be great-hearted in the coiled
dimensions.

There is no suspension
of deep love

and
YOU

are
YOU

and
the body of
your dyad, your marriage.

NARCISSUS WAKING UP

IT IS LOVELY TO BE THE EMBODYING
and to adore my
S
E
L
F
— a flower now

flamboyant

in the dark whirlpool
of scintillating anxieties
shining with silver
edges.

The smell of raspberries
is friends at the door
and
I

LOVE
THIS

it is all mine

from the unknown dimensions
to
the
splinter-shatter
of bosons

to the bare flesh
under the quilt

ALL CHILDREN

REMBRANDT   RAPHAEL   LORCA
& SU T'UNG-PO
are children of messiah
children themselves
like sponges, single-cell beings, and storms
FROM
AN
ORIGINAL

P
R
I
M
E

CAUSE, coming together
space-twitching
making fantasies
like me
in this gorgeousness
of no proportions or scale

Just a sunny day
over
the loud-roaring ocean
and the murmur of petroleum

INTIMATE JOURNALS

INTIMATE JOURNALS means that
even a Bozo
M
U
S
T
study compassion
to feel with others' senses

YOU ARE SO DEEP AND BRIGHT

I
WOULD
overflow everything
and wrap you in myself
flowing into you

GATES
OPEN

I pour out
A
S
T
O
N
I
S
H
E
D
shed of miracles
astounded as a quasar
letting it happen

WET BLACK ROCK

NO WORRY, THE REALMS ARE INTER-PENETRABLE
ARE CONTINGENT
and multiple
Forget it
— it is all water
in water — as we are ten trillion
creatures in each wave
of a miracle as it crashes

into ordinary surfs of neon and laughs
and ascends into trails
of sky-flying pelicans. WE ARE BLESSED
and damned by this grab bag of senses.
Aching with the joy of it

feeling nothing but the surge carrying forward
and all the way back
knowing we are the non-beginning

and the extreme common edges
like those sandpipers
by the wet black rock
and your dazzling sunlit shoulder

Forget it. It is all o.k. We are present
or not
in shades of forever

WATER IN WATER

"THE ANIMAL IS IN THE WORLD
LIKE WATER IN WATER"
— there is no tension of time in living tension.
A mammal not a flower!
Not a rose or violet but able
to build love and hold qualia
together in bursts in many zones:

in
CAR REPAIR SHOP
or
WATERFALL

and to GESTURE
not communicate
OUT-SPEAKING, ENACTING
the nearest edge of the dance —

dying or devouring or pissing
on a patch of moss or white toilet bowl
or tv screen.
A MAMMAL NOT A FLOWER!
Passing in no time

PRESENT
IN
NO
TIME

with no fur of molecules
or stardust

alive
in living tension

like water in water

(quote from Scalapino and Bataille)

FRANK AND VIVIANA

PROTEAN WARS AND LOVES OF LIVING STARDUST
are the descant that the FLESH BODY
dances to, as it hurls grenades
and valentines, brightening synapses
in the expanding cortex. Never free us from ourselves.
We are the endless model. No beginning —
ribosomes and archaea chains
becoming mammals. Cortex, skin, and eyes
and ears. Finger soles. No holes
anywhere — all breathing. Speaking
in growing neural constellations.
Friends glow
with selves. It begins with tenderness to the layer
holding breath with spasms. Set free, liberated by a
nanosecond's flicker.

Touches are deeds and actions of star matter.
THE SCENT OF THE BODY'S NOSES.
Not roses, but touches make life's odor

in

flesh-freedom
debouching here

floating on gravity

THE JUDITH POEM
for Judith Malina

JUDITH, YOU WROTE,
"I COULD WALK OUT INTO THE WORLD
LIKE GAUTAMA
AND ENCOUNTER DEATH, DISEASE & OLD AGE,
AND DECIDE TO SAVE THE WORLD,"
and you saved it. Standing naked on the stage with arms
stretched like a star you shouted out your conquered fear and
bravery: *"Poetry is politics."* You created an antipolitics
verifying the Shelleys,
so much like you and Julian
with your white-shouldered trembling soul.

Your actions shape the energy.
for a revolution of peace and brave action.

You are the dark bird in a golden surf
of lovers — an osprey with scarlet beak
in the surge of body philosophers
you helped to free. You and the Living Theater
turn many from the prisoning walls of dead horses.
Away from grim outrages
of Tiananmen, Gallipoli, and Feluja,
into bodies of awakened meat-spirit
to be revolutionaries and actors in the street.
They cry out and march against
the wars of cybernetic armaments, murdering suicides
and suiciding murderers

Now we outnumber those who hate imagination,
and whose poison is for inspiration.

PEOPLE ARE AWAKENED!

What you do stands us beside Kropotkin and Goldman,
with di Prima and Chez.
You have unleashed
the radiance of the loving,
deep mammal spirit of women and men,
alchemized it;
and let it be active light and the sparkling and laughing
rage of genius.
Your art and your directing have breathed shapeliness,
created a breathing,
which has seen
paradiso now in the streets by the millions

You wrote: "Regard the tip of your forefinger,
pointing it toward your eyes."

See that you are innocent and free
to act and to cry out in the cities and theaters.

For seventy years the Living Theater has brought
a revolution
nearer for all
no other gestural social action has pointed as far
NOR LASTED AS LONG.
Would the Occupy Movement have happened without
your energy and your struggle for social change
and out-roar in the cities?
Children may not know
the names of their grandparents.

For three generations and ongoing,
theater dust has churned on stages and main streets.
Artaud knew that theater will be brought alive
AS AN ORGANISM
TO BREATHE AND PROCREATE.

Memories of resistance actions and for social change
are obliterated by the state
whether Stalin's state or North America's or Mao's state.
How often Judith, have you performed
inside jails and prisons
in factories, in court houses, and embassies?
How many times were you and the troupe busted and jailed?
Forced out and driven from cities and countries.
Your Living Theater has created more than a hundred plays
from *The Brig* to *The Money Tower*,
to *Antigone*, and *Frankenstein*.

YOUR
OWN
WILD TRIBE
of children, parents, and elders!

And more being born
who will wake from entertainments
and nodding-off of this decade
to become your multi-hued lovers and your children.

COLOR FIELD
for Terry Riley

ONE MORE CHERUB IN HONEY
SNOW LEOPARD IN AMBER
GROWLING AS MARK ROTHKO DIES
THE SURGE SETTLING SHAPING SMOOTH STONES
COUNTLESS AS NEURON SPARKS IN LIGHT MATTER

TRIUMPHAL BEYOND DEATH

AS

A

FLICKER MOTH

COLIBRI

FLASH IMAGE

OF
ALWAYS STUFF
PHYSIS IN TRANSIT
to being

BEING
a pearl

PEARL
OF
NOTHING
NECTAR

JUST
SO

CHERUB IN HONEY

SNOW LEOPARD

SONG HEAVY

LAST BREATH POEM:

After watching human
efforts to save the beached
pilot whale at Rockport, MA.
Many times the large dolphin
reversed their efforts and
returned to the strand.

TWO TON QUALIA-BEING:

globe head

SPIKE TEETH

all being-receptors

RECEPTORS
CONCEIVED
BY
QUALIA
a
l
i
v
e

LIVING

resonation

x~X~X~x

MEAT

RED-BLACK

inside
is

every where

RESONATING

slick black
on
sea edge

...'...'.'"..
;;; ;;; ; ;;

MOEBIUS
BULK
BREATHING
HULK

this way

OF
LIFE

CEDING

IS
IT

the way

CON
SCIOUS
NESS

VAST

HEART

ALL BODY

SHAPE

songheavy

VOICE

to imagine

self-spired

SPOUTED

i
n
s
p
i
r
e
d

death-self

(DEATH SELF)

FREE

to swim
in
non-ever
FOR
EVER
all
bright

AFIRE

five trillion per nanosecond

neuron linking

in the POD

WHAT THREAT —

OR FEAR
— OR
DISEASE
— OR
﹖﹖

LEADS NO WAY

to
follow

we laugh
together in the torch

of wetwave darkness

nothing

NOTHING NESS

needs
this
LIFE

and
now

we are gone

A
TOOTHED
SMILE

SMILE

IN
THE

WAVE
LAP

———
———

THIS
PROUD

RED AND BLACK

———

MEAT
LOVE

HEARING-VOICE

TREMBLING

TO GO

Michael McClure is an award-winning American poet, playwright, songwriter, and novelist. A key figure of the Beat Generation, McClure is immortalized as Pat McLear in Jack Kerouac's novels *The Dharma Bums* and *Big Sur*. He also participated in the '60s counterculture alongside musicians like Janis Joplin and Jim Morrison. McClure remains active as a poet, essayist, and playwright, and lives with his wife, Amy, in the San Francisco Bay Area.